CHASING PLEASURE
WITH PAIN

HAYWOOD ROBINSON

CHASING PLEASURE WITH PAIN

Charleston, SC
www.PalmettoPublishing.com

Chasing Pleasure with Pain

First Edition

Hardcover ISBN: 978-1-64990-954-1
Paperback ISBN: 978-1-64990-943-5
eBook ISBN: 978-1-64990-621-2

Dedication

I am dedicating this book to my mother. Without her, this book would not be a reality. She has been my rock, my biggest supporter, and my closest ally throughout many stages of my life. She always saw my potential and encouraged me to write my truth. Thank you, Mom. I love you.

Foreword

Mental illness is not a choice. No one chooses to outwardly appear to be lazy or unreasonable or paranoid. No one wakes up one day and decides to have illogical thoughts and disruptive reactions. These are symptoms of an illness that is no more preventable than any other illness. When I began exhibiting the symptoms of my mental illness in my teens, my parents sent me to a behavioral modification school in Montana. They did not think for even a moment that my behavior was a product of a debilitating illness. Mental health wasn't spoken of in the late '90s. Unfortunately, the school they sent me to broke me down emotionally and mentally by using attack therapy and humiliation. The combination of mental illness and the trauma inflicted by this program led to me leading a tragic life for another fifteen years. Even after my diagnosis, the struggle was different but just as difficult. I want parents who read this book to consider the mental health of their child before entrusting and signing over 51 percent custody to complete strangers. I also want people who suffer from mental illness to know they are not alone, that their feelings are valid, and that they matter.

Chapter 1

This Is Why I Don't Come to School

"Haywood, come with me please," Vice Principal Mr. Wilson said from the doorway of the classroom.

I leaned over to grab my bookbag while turning around to face my best friend, La, and said, "This is why I don't come to school."

It was October of 2000, and I was a senior in high school. I hadn't been to school in over a week. I couldn't muster the strength to leave my bed most mornings, and when I was awake, I only wanted to self-medicate with marijuana and alcohol. The attention from my boyfriend was a drug in itself. I had run away from home and had been staying with him, because I didn't want anything to do with my parents and their rules. I had no idea at the time that I was attempting to escape from severe mental illness.

I followed Mr. Wilson to the principal's office, where I found my aunt Betsy speaking with the principal.

"Hi, Aunt Betsy. What are you doing here?" I asked quizzically.

"Hi, Mary Haywood! We just haven't spent any time together recently, and your principal has agreed to let me take you to lunch. I'll bring you back right afterward," my aunt said in a nervous but enthusiastic tone.

Looking back, I don't think I had much choice, but I hated school, so any excuse to leave was fine by me. We went to TGI Friday's, and I ate a turkey croissant sandwich. Once we finished up, we got into her dark blue Toyota Sequoia and began driving again. However, we weren't going toward the school; we were going toward her house.

"Where are we going?" I asked.

"I forgot I needed to grab something from home before dropping you off," she said nonchalantly.

This made me a little curious, but there was no way I could've predicted what was coming. When we arrived at her house, I saw my dad's green Ford Explorer in the driveway, and a red van I had never seen before was parked out front. When we pulled into the driveway, my aunt rolled down my window so my dad could stick his head in and open the door from the inside.

"These people are going to take you to a place where you'll get better," my dad said solemnly.

It was at this time that I saw the middle-aged couple. The man said, "We can do this the easy way or the hard way." They took me by each of my arms and led me to their van.

"What the fuck are you doing? Let go of me! Dad, I hate you! You can't do this, I'm seventeen!" I screamed at the top of my lungs along with many other profanities and expletives.

I don't remember much of the trip, but I do remember we had an overnight layover somewhere, so we had to stay in a hotel. I'm with complete strangers (a husband-and-wife team), and we were in a room with two beds, one of which they pushed against the door so I couldn't escape in the middle of the night. They weren't supposed to, but they let me call my parents.

"Please, Mom! Please let me come home! I swear I'll be good! I will do exactly what you want me to. I'll go to school. I'll make straight As. I promise I'll be good, *please!*"

My mother was broken. She could barely speak. "I love you, Haywood. This place will be good for you. We've researched it, and it has good results. We're doing this because we love you."

The following day I arrived in Thompson Falls, Montana, at a behavioral modification school named Spring Creek Lodge. I arrived at night, and I did "intake" in a trailer at the bottom of campus.

"Go behind the curtain and strip down," said an overweight woman with a deep, authoritative voice. I did as I was told as the couple drove away. I was terrified.

They went through my jeans and my pink sweater and bra to make sure I wasn't hiding drugs. They threw my underwear out because it was a thong, which was contraband, and they took the shoelaces out of my purple and pink Skechers.

"All right, get dressed," said the woman as she handed back my clothes.

It had to have been around zero to ten degrees outside with snow on the ground, and the only jacket I had was an old ski jacket from eighth grade that my parents had packed for me in a blue and white Roxy suitcase (which I still use to this day).

I was escorted to the second floor of a wood cabin from outside stairs. The door opened, and I had an out of body experience. I watched myself walk into the room with a terrified look on my face. My hair was wavy and stringy from washing it the night before without being able to blow dry it. I wanted nothing to do with any of them. I was not like them. Truth is, I didn't know who I was anymore.

Chapter 2

Spring Creek Lodge

"*Lights on!*"

We had five minutes to have both feet on the floor and another five minutes to have our beds made immaculately with no pieces of our blankets hanging down anywhere. Once that was done, we had five minutes to take a shower, starting as soon as the water turned on. Once we got changed, we had an additional five minutes to organize the three laundry baskets that held all of our belongings. They checked our baskets before forcing us to stand in a heel-to-toe line at the door. Then we would get patted down, to make sure we weren't bringing anything with us and to make sure we only had on two layers of clothing. Even though the winters were brutal, any more than two layers of clothing was considered preparing to run, and you would get a category five consequence for being a "run risk." There was always a junior staff student who would accompany the family mothers to help enforce these rules. You became junior staff by getting a certain number of points and completing the seminars.

We would walk in this heel-toe line to our classroom, where we did self-learning. We would read each chapter of our textbooks and take the tests from our textbooks. It wasn't exactly a quality education. After class we'd line up again to get patted down, and then it was off to the cafeteria, which was called the Hungry Horse. It was oatmeal every morning, and you could only get sweetener if you were a Level Two or higher. Level Ones got no condiments or sweeteners. Once we went through the line and got our food, we sat as a family and listened to self-help tapes with speakers like Zig Ziglar and Tony Robbins.

We only had twenty minutes to eat before we were up in our heel-toe line getting patted down, and then it was off to exercise, which mostly consisted of us sitting on the basketball court or doing boot camp exercise drills, depending on who was in charge that day. It was basically the same thing over and over. Heel-toe, pat down, off to class or cafeteria.

At the end of the day, we had "Group," where we would share and get feedback regarding our day or what we learned about ourselves. After that, we would write "reflections" of the day, and we would get points based on these writings. The days went by so slowly, and the lights were out by 10:00 p.m.

Talking was almost never allowed without permission. No talking in line, no talking in class, no talking in the cafeteria, no talking in the bathrooms, no talking to people in another room from you. The only time we were allowed to talk to each other was the short amount of time before we went to bed. Even then, Level Ones weren't allowed to talk to Level Twos, so even when we were allowed to talk, we were very restricted in whom we could talk to.

We were also incentivized to tell on each other. So if my friend whispered something to me in line, I'd get points if I referred her for a "talking on silence." I'd also be recognized as "working the program." We would sometimes be put on silence for days at a time, either individually or as a family.

That meant you couldn't talk, nor could anyone else talk to or even acknowledge you. This was a challenge I was put on quite frequently because I was constantly being accused of being an "attention suck" and being loud and acting out for a reaction. This type of treatment is torture for a developing mind. To this day, I am triggered by being shushed or by being told to be quiet.

Every so often, we'd be woken up in the middle of the night with loud band music and made to do challenges, which were either physical labor or some form of humiliation. People who didn't follow the rules were sent to "the Hobbit," which was an isolation cabin with nothing but a foam mat. I heard horrible noises attributed to abuse coming from that cabin. I was terrified of being sent there, and thankfully I never was.

By the second or third week, I thought I had this place figured out and finally shared in Group. "I see now how much hell I put my parents through. I was so spoiled and selfish and didn't appreciate all of the sacrifices my parents made for me. I will work the program and make my parents proud."

"Well, you sure got the jargon down. Too bad none of that was genuine. You are completely fake, and you need to be humbled." I was immediately called out by a girl who had really drunk the program Kool-Aid. This was going to be tougher than I thought.

Day after day, I listened to these girls, but there was something I just wasn't understanding. They all said the same things, like "How did you create that for yourself?" and "Way to be accountable." Where was all of this coming from? I found out in my first seminar, Discovery.

Chapter 3

Seminars

Getting through these seminars was mandatory to be able to graduate the program and go home. The last thing any of these kids wanted was to be told to "choose out." This was a term they used for kicking us out of the seminar. However, we had to take accountability for what happened to us, so instead of them saying they were kicking us out, they told us we were "choosing out" by not reacting to the exercises the way they wanted us to. I still have much of these seminars blocked out, but I remember being in a group of my peers with the junior staff (fellow program kids on the higher levels), adult staff, and a facilitator.

"What's the worst thing that has ever happened to you?" asked a junior staff girl. The way she asked was venomous. It was like she was waiting for me to say the wrong thing, which made me even more petrified to answer.

Everyone was looking at me. The first thing that came to mind was being sexually assaulted by a Citadel Cadet at age fifteen.

"I was at a Halloween party two years ago, dressed up as Julia Roberts from Pretty Woman. These Citadel Cadets crashed the party, and one of them fed me multiple beer funnels then asked me to take a walk with him. He led me into a neighbor's bushes. I was forced to perform oral sex on him." I told the story very detached. The only way I could get through this was by removing myself from the emotion.

The facilitator was amused, as if he had been there and caught me in a lie. "Wrong! It is obvious that was not the extent of your assault. Something else happened that night, and until you can tell us the real story, you'll have to choose out of this seminar. Think about what truly happened that night, and come back next time." They didn't believe me. They did not believe that was the extent of my assault. I was dumbfounded.

That assault *was* the worst thing that had happened to me, which I later came to understand was awful in its own right, but since it wasn't enough, I would be prepared next time.

"I was led upstairs by the Citadel Cadet. We started making out, then he put his hand up my skirt. I asked him to stop, but he grabbed both of my wrists in his hand and held them above my head against the headboard while he penetrated me. It felt like a lifetime, but then it was finally over. He pulled his pants up and walked out of the room." I deserved an Oscar in that seminar room that day. I said all of this with such conviction. Remember, I was acting for my life. I couldn't go home if I didn't make it through these seminars, and I wasn't making it through Discovery without a jaw-dropping story.

Later on in the seminar, I was made to bang a towel wrapped in duct tape on the floor while I screamed at my "rapist."

Junior staff boys yelled in my face. "You're a dirty whore! You're a little slut! You deserved this! You were asking for this!"

At one point, one of them pushed a pillow against me, simulating the pressure of my rapist while I continued to yell at them. "I'm worthy! I'm not dirty! I'm not a slut!"

I left that seminar changed forever. I spent the rest of the program retelling that story over and over again, to the point that I even believed it myself. I retold this story in therapy for ten years before I came to terms with the fact that this story was not my truth. I left that seminar broken. So broken. The whole point of these seminars was to break you down so that they can build you up to the cookie cutter version of yourself that your parents always wanted you to be, to take accountability for why things happened to you. I even took responsibility for my own "rape." "How did you create this for yourself?" was common program lingo.

Another exercise was "Lifeboat," where we had to go around to everyone in the room and tell them "You die," or "You're worthy of being saved." (I'm not sure if this is the exact phrasing, but I definitely remember saying and being told "You die.") There were only a certain number of spots on the proverbial lifeboat. In the same exercise, you'd have to say a person's name or tell them they weren't important enough to remember if you didn't know their name. I remember there was a lot of peer voting happening in these seminars. Most of the time, we'd have to stand on a chair as a group of our male and female peers rated us and voted on our worth and gave us "feedback" about our character. It was humiliating. There were literally dozens of exercises like this. These are just the ones I vaguely remember.

In my survivor groups, others speak of much worse psychologically torturous exercises we went through, and while it might ring a tiny bell deep in my subconscious, my brain refuses to fully reveal the repressed memories in an attempt to protect myself. I can only imagine how much worse it got, because the trauma lives inside me and is released in a multitude of ways: physically, emotionally, in the decisions I make, and so on. It's also important to note that these seminars lasted from around 6:00 a.m. to about 10:00 or 11:00 p.m., and once you got to your cabin, you were "on silence," yet still had hours of writing homework to do for the following day in the seminar. We were fed very little during this time. They deprived us and broke us down, because a broken down, hungry, and sleep-deprived child is very easy to manipulate and brainwash.

Chapter 4

Daddy Issues

One day while I was in the classroom, someone came through the door and called my name, said I had a phone call. This was most unexpected, because I had dropped from a Level Three, which is the level you're required to be at to receive phone calls. Anyone who got a phone call while not at level three or higher was usually receiving very bad news from back home. I immediately got a lump in my throat.

"Hello?" I was excited to speak to my parents but still very nervous about the possible reason.

"Hi, Haywood. Your mother and I are both on the phone," my dad said carefully, as if he were speaking to a little child.

"What's going on? I'm not on the right level to get a call, so what is wrong?"

"Your mother and I are separated, and we're getting a divorce," he said, sounding relieved to have finally gotten it over with.

Tears began welling up in my eyes. I couldn't speak, because when I try to speak while crying, I just cry harder.

In the absence of a response, my dad continued. "I wrote you a letter that explains it in full, but we wanted to tell you this over the phone."

"Mom? Is this true?" She had been completely silent.

"It is, Haywood. Please don't let this derail your progress. We're so proud of you, and we will be fine at home." She didn't sound like herself. She sounded very distant.

Then my case manager abruptly ended the phone call.

Sure enough, a few days later I got a letter from my father. My therapist said I could pick one friend for company, read it in his office, and stay in his building for the rest of the day, just to process everything. I didn't keep the letter, so I cannot remember word for word, but basically my father admitted to having an affair, and that was why they were getting a divorce. I was devastated. This moment shaped so much of my life. My father and I had never bonded. We didn't *not* get along, but I just don't think he knew how to be a father on an emotional level. He always provided for our family. He always joked around with me and came to the sporting events (the ones he was able to make when he wasn't traveling), but an actual bond never formed. But while we never bonded, I did hold him on a pedestal, and in hindsight I never really felt good enough for him to sincerely bond with me. Now he was letting me down so deeply. I believe my borderline personality disorder (BPD) solidified in this moment.

Chapter 5

Borderline Personality Disorder

Borderline personality disorder is something that happens from not forming a bond with one of your parents. It is an illness marked by an ongoing pattern of varying moods and behaviors as well as fluctuating self-image beliefs. These symptoms often result in impulsive actions and problems in relationships.

People with BPD may experience mood swings and display uncertainty about how they see themselves and their role in the world. As a result, their interests and values can change quickly. People with BPD also tend to view things in extremes, such as all good or all bad. Their opinions of other people can also change quickly. An individual who is viewed as a friend one day may be considered an enemy or traitor the next. These shifting feelings can lead to intense and unstable relationships.[1] This, especially coupled with bipolar disorder, is detrimental to anyone.

1. "Borderline Personality Disorder," National Institute of Mental Health, accessed [September, 20, 2020], https://www.nimh.nih.gov/health/topics/borderline-personality-disorder/index.shtml.

These two illnesses, which would not be diagnosed for nearly fifteen more years, would slowly corrode my quality of life like acid. There were literally no licensed medical professionals on the Spring Creek Lodge campus to deal with mental illness at this program. Mental illness was seen as laziness or defiance, which we were solely responsible for. Attack therapy and humiliation was their answer.

Chapter 6

Toxicity

By the time I went home, I was so brainwashed that, when I began to inevitably experience signs of my mood and personality disorders, I thought it was all my fault. After I graduated high school, my mom pulled me from the program. I had turned eighteen while I was in the program, but I was far away in Montana, and I had nowhere to go if I left. Once home, I attended Trident Technical College for a semester before transferring to the College of Charleston. I was so lost. My mom allowed me to see my friend La again, but that was only after I convinced her that *I* was the bad influence and not the other way around.

On July 4, 2002, La and I went to the beach and ran into a guy we had gone to high school with. I had always had a little crush on him, but he had always had a girlfriend. We ended up making out that night and sleeping in the same bed together. We were literally inseparable from that moment on. I spent all of my time with him. He was really the only thing that mattered to me. I moved into a dorm with La, but I spent most nights at his apartment.

After the first year at the College of Charleston, we moved in together. Shortly thereafter, I began failing my classes, and my relationship became extremely toxic. We drank too much and fought over everything. We were both extremely jealous, and we began resenting each other. Our fights frequently got physical. We both fought violently. In one incident, he stomped my face into the tile of a hotel room bathroom. I escaped and ran to the front desk to call the police. He was charged with criminal domestic violence.

I was experiencing so many emotions at the time. I went on benders where I would party for multiple nights in a row, which would fuel his jealousy. These episodes were always followed with debilitating bouts of depression. It was around this time that I began cutting myself. Sometimes it was a cry for help, and other times it was just to control my pain.

Chapter 7

The Party Never Ends

This boyfriend and I finally broke up, but we were on and off for many years after. I eventually dropped out of college and got a job as a cocktail waitress at a local bar. This bar frequently had live music, which is something I'm very passionate about. I slept with one of the musicians, and this is when I became addicted to intimacy with men. It wasn't necessarily the sex but the attention I was infatuated with. I began to dabble in cocaine use and lost a ton of weight. I became extremely promiscuous. I would go home with a different musician or bar patron every night.

One day it dawned on me that I couldn't remember the last time I'd had my period. I took a test, and sure enough, I was pregnant. I was terrified, mortified, and deeply ashamed. One of the bartenders I was very close to offered to loan me the money to get an abortion. I'm not condoning abortion as a form of birth control, but I was severely ill. I was not thinking about my future or how I would feel about this decision down the road.

We pulled up to Planned Parenthood, and there were protesters picketing out front. That's when I began crying, and I didn't stop until I got back home. I walked in and felt a stronger feeling of shame with every step. My mind kept going back to Montana. "You're a slut! You're a dirty whore!" I began to feel like I was fulfilling that prophecy.

It wasn't so much painful as it was frighteningly uncomfortable and demoralizing. The doctor and nurse showed no emotion. No one held my hand. I just squeezed my eyes shut and waited for the noise to stop. I will remember the noise the suction made for the rest of my life. There isn't a single time when I don't think about that moment if I find out a friend is pregnant or see pregnancy depicted onscreen. I always wonder what could have been.

Am I a monster? It doesn't help that people feel so comfortable shoving their own beliefs down your throat. The pro-lifers are not saying anything about someone who gets an abortion that I haven't already thought of myself. I still struggle with this. I don't know who the father was, so I couldn't tell him, and I also had no one waiting for me when I got home. I sat by myself in the dark for days before going back to work. I didn't last long there, as my behavioral antics got the best of me. I had sex in the parking lot. I got wasted on the clock. I was late almost every day. My mom finally stepped in and made me take a hard look at myself.

Chapter 8

Suicide Round One

My mother works for a large corporation and frequently travels for work. Through her connections, she managed to get me an interview to work the front desk at a swanky historic hotel in downtown Charleston. I charmed my way through the interview and got the job. I had gained a lot of weight since the abortion, and I continued to gain weight. I still partied, but I built a wall of fat between me and any potential man who might be interested in me sexually.

I was good at this job. I was good at faking it, anyway, and that was all I needed to pay my bills and buy my food. After working for a year at this hotel, I had an in with another historic hotel downtown, and I interviewed for the front office supervisor position and got it.

I hadn't yet started in this position when I survived my first suicide attempt. I truly hated myself. I couldn't stand to look at myself in the mirror. I had pushed most of my good friends away. I was either constantly partying or constantly depressed. The depression was so deep, I couldn't live with it anymore. I wanted it to end. I needed to escape the dark hole that my life had become. So one night, I took a bottle full of depression medication, as ironic as that is, and wrote a suicide note. As soon as I was done writing the note, I regretted it. I left my room and woke up a friend who was sleeping on my couch. I told her what had happened, and she took me to the hospital. As soon as I got there, they made me drink liquid charcoal to harden the medication so it wouldn't seep into my bloodstream.

I called my mom, and she was there in the blink of an eye. She was so concerned, so confused. She felt like my life was a reflection on her, so she took these things personally. She covered for me by calling my new job, and she got me a week off. Once I was stable, the doctor sat me in a wheelchair, cuffed my wrists, and put a blanket over me to hide the handcuffs. This was standard procedure. I'm not sure if it still is, but it shouldn't be, because you're just punishing the victim and shaming them even further. They then transported me to the psychiatric ward of the Medical University of South Carolina. This was my first stay at a psych ward, and it felt eerily similar to when I was dropped off in Montana. My life was beginning to form cycles of stability and instability. I was diagnosed with depression and prescribed more antidepressants, but they never truly helped me.

Chapter 9

Seattle

While the drugs never helped, I somehow managed to live day to day, never knowing which Haywood I'd wake up to. I would pray to be the Haywood that was motivated and happy, but when I wasn't, it was devastating. However, I would cover it up with lies. So many lies. I've missed people's weddings, christenings, birthdays, and a lot of work. That was always tricky. I always had to have a different excuse, and it had to be good. That's why when I make an excuse today, I'm nervous and afraid people will think I'm lying.

Anyway, a close friend from college had moved to Seattle once she graduated and encouraged me to move out there. I had survived my suicide attempt and had been free of dangerous suicidal thoughts for almost a year, so I figured this was as good a time as any to get out of Charleston and see what else was out there. I ended up landing a job as a front desk manager at a popular hotel in downtown Seattle and moving in with a friend of a friend.

What I didn't know when I accepted the job was that I would have to work the night shift for the first six months. By the time I found out, I had already moved there, and there weren't a ton of jobs available. So there I was, living in a city where I knew practically no one and could barely get to know anyone because of my schedule. My friend from college was amazing and invited me to so many events with all of her Seattle friends, but I could already feel the depression settling back in, the deep depression with the accompanying suicidal thoughts.

To add insult to injury, a dear friend of mine in Charleston received devastating news that she had stage 4 melanoma. This was Rina, the sister of one of my best friends, Christina. Rina was one of the most inspiring and radiant people I had ever met, and she was literally dying while I was on the other side of the country.

While I experienced some amazing times in Seattle, especially the music scene, I needed to come home to Charleston. I was aching to be closer to my friends and family. I honestly really missed my mom. I hate being far away from her to this day. I can literally feel when she's physically far from me. She has been the only constant in my life. I've pushed so many people out, but she has never wavered. So after a year in Seattle, I came home.

Chapter 10

Human Bulldozer

While I was away, I had really beefed up my resume, so I was able to get a great job as an assistant general manager at a popular hotel chain. While I was good at my job, I was in and out of depression and mania so often that I had to make a lot of excuses for my tardiness and absences. I'm not really sure how I continued to hide my mental illness. I truly thought I was simply lazy and impulsive and that I had created this for myself. These were all points that were driven into my brain at the program in Montana. They would be a constant echo in my head for decades.

It's hard to admit to having a mental illness, yes, but it's much harder to admit you're just lazy and inconsiderate. That's what I assumed I was, just a bad person. This is why I kept these feelings a secret and always had to be on top of my lies. I carried on like this, just keeping my head above water, for another year or so. I didn't fall apart again until Tom.

Tom (which is not his real name) was a married man I met through a professional networking event. We had a one-night stand that turned into much more. I knew he was married, and I was disgusted with myself. My dad had cheated on my mom, and I despised this fact. I think it was the self-loathing that caused my next spiral.

Tom controlled me. If I didn't hear from him, I would get a sickening feeling, and I would lose my mind. In an attempt to avoid these feelings, I would drink a bottle or two of wine a day. That would only fuel my depression until, like clockwork, my mania kicked in to finish off whatever semblance of normalcy I had left that my depression hadn't already wrecked. Then Tom would swoop in, and we would stay in a hotel for a night, and I would live for those nights. He lived about an hour away, and this would only happen once a week. If he skipped a week, I'd lose it.

After a while, he stopped springing for hotels and would just come to my apartment on his way home to have sex with me then leave some cash on the counter. I felt like a prostitute. I guess I kind of was. He would throw money at me every time I got out of control and threatened to kill myself or tell his wife. When the visits from Tom became few and far between, I started seeing another guy named Tyler.

Tyler (also not *his* real name) didn't want to date me either. In fact, he flat-out told me, "I would date you if you had your shit together." My illness was preventing people from loving me, but again, I just thought no one loved me because I was a shitty human. On the nights I couldn't see Tyler, I would also have a full-blown panic attack. These relationship issues were directly related to my BPD. If you weren't with me, you were against me. And not just against me but actively out to get me. The worst part about this was the fact that I sabotaged relationships with people who truly did care about me.

My best friend since high school, La, had finally had enough. We had gone on a girls' trip to Savannah, and I went home with some stranger, and she was rightfully worried sick all night to the point that she couldn't even enjoy her trip. When she voiced her concern the following morning, I just let her have it. I lashed out at her as if she were my mortal enemy. She was finally tired of being my punching bag and stopped communicating with me all together.

I found out later that La's mother was dying of cancer. I will never forget when I found out. I was at my surprise thirtieth birthday party, and my friend Christina told me the news. I proceeded to text La (pretending I didn't know) to see if she was coming to my party. I was more concerned about myself and her being my friend than I was about her mother and her own emotional state.

I realize now that was delusional thinking and an impulsive response. I also think I was probably in deep denial because I was extremely close to her mother in my teen years and my early twenties. I try not to make myself feel guilty, but this continues to be one of the hardest things to forgive myself for. This wasn't the only time I had pushed away someone who cared about me. I continued to ruin relationships in dramatic and grandiose ways by simply being a human bulldozer, but this one *really* hurt—probably both of us, if I had to guess. She could have really used my support during this time, but I wasn't there for her.

I have tried time and again to reassure myself that I, too, was sick and did not have the capacity to be there for anyone else.

Chapter 11

And the Party Continues

After that spiral, I was consequently fired from my job and evicted from my apartment. I got a job as a waitress at a bar I frequented, and thus began my two-year manic spiral. Sure, I got depressed, as per usual, but the mania is what really kept me going for those two years. I moved into a rat-infested hoarder's house downtown, where I rarely actually stayed. Not sober anyway.

Once again, I began acting promiscuous, going home with different men almost nightly. I couch- and bed-hopped, avoiding that house like the plague. It didn't matter, because, like I said, I spent most nights out. I would party every single night. I had pushed every true friend away and stopped communicating with them altogether. My parents had no idea what to do. My mom tried to save me, but it was no use. I had to be out. I had to receive attention from men. This was not what I wanted. It was what I *needed*. Eventually, the inevitable happened.

I couldn't remember when I had last had a period, so I took a pregnancy test, and sure enough, it was positive. I panicked. Once again, I had no clue who the father was, although I had a pretty good idea. I was extremely unstable and truthfully out of my mind, consistently manic. I called my mom at 4:00 a.m. the next morning. I told her I was going to find a family to put me up until I had the baby, and then they could have it. I couldn't have another abortion. I told myself I would never do that again—I couldn't handle it emotionally.

However, my mother reminded me that I also couldn't handle a pregnancy at that time. I could barely take care of myself. I kept myself clean and fed, but outside of that, I took on zero additional responsibilities. I routinely paid my rent late. I got my license suspended for not paying for insurance. I paid zero bills outside of my cell phone bill. My mom told me she would pay for me to get an abortion and that we needed to visit the clinic immediately.

It was earlier in the pregnancy this time, so instead of surgery, they simply gave me some pills to take that would cause a miscarriage. I'm truly not sure what is worse, hearing the suction of life leaving your body or watching life slowly evacuate from your body over the course of twenty-four hours.

Thank God my mom was with me every second of it. I stayed in her bed that night, and she consoled me every time I went to the bathroom. Each visit was draining the life from me. I felt like I was losing my soul. My level of self-hatred was at an all-time high.

Chapter 12

The Diagnosis

It wasn't long after the miscarriage that I began bartending instead of waiting tables, which offered more money but fewer hours. This gave me the opportunity to actually reflect on my life and how I could get it back on track. I began seeing a psychiatrist and therapist whom my friend had recommended.

She was different than any other psychiatrist I had ever seen before, which is saying a lot, since I've seen a ton. She didn't rush the session. She took time to ask me questions and try to understand me and my symptoms. When she first told me I had both bipolar disorder and borderline personality disorder, I was crushed. I literally felt all of the air leave the room. Everything tightened, and my eyes instantly overflowed. I couldn't grasp the concept of living the rest of my life with this dirty secret.

However, once I began researching these illnesses, it was quite validating to realize that, for my whole life, my thoughts and actions had been symptoms. I was not lazy. I was not a shitty human. I was severely ill for twenty years, and I had *no idea!*

We immediately started experimenting with medication to find the right combinations. I began to stabilize within a few weeks. It was incredible. It felt like magic.

Chapter 13

A New Leaf

One day, one of my regulars at the bar told me she had a job for me at a start-up apparel company if I was interested. I was ecstatic. I had plenty of customer service experience, and all I had to do was take care of these customers and their orders. It was nine to five, Monday through Friday, and a decent salary. It wasn't as much as I was making bartending, but I poured most of my tips back into the bar every shift anyway, with all the drinks I bought.

My first priority was getting out of that house downtown. I had been talking to a guy on Facebook, whom I thought I was in love with, and he helped me move into a tiny studio apartment in West Ashley. He lived a couple of hours away and claimed his car had recently been totaled, so when we met up with each other, I'd go pick him up and bring him to Charleston.

Sometimes I'd stay with him at his parents' house. His parents were lovely. I adored his mom, but there were a million red flags when it came to her son. Just like every other guy, I acted overdependent, but he gaslit me into thinking I was the only one doing anything wrong in the relationship, even though we were living 100 percent on my dime, and I just wanted him to spend time with me. I don't know, maybe that breakup was my fault. Either way, it ended, and it was for the best.

A few days after he left me, I got an adorable senior dog named Layla. She saved my life. I probably would have killed myself if I didn't have Layla. Having a dog to care for gave me a purpose. I struggled with my job, but overall it was great for its steady paycheck, and I was good at it. One day while I was at work, Layla got into my Ibuprofen and overdosed. I hadn't cried like that in years. I was *scream* crying. It was awful. The very next weekend, I adopted my three-legged angel, Banjo. I like to say that Layla rescued me, and I rescued Banjo. He came from a terribly abusive situation, and he was super skittish. Life was ok.

Chapter 14

First My Mind, Now My Body

B anjo and I were living a drama free life and I was fairly happy. I was going to work regularly and while it was very stressful, I was handling it. Or so I thought. One day after I got home from work I started to feel strange. I got a splitting headache and when I tried to speak, it felt like my tongue was as big as my mouth. I couldn't articulate words. The severity of this symptom lasted for a matter of minutes before I was able to speak somewhat clearly again. I brushed it off and just thought it was a freak thing. The following day at work, I still didn't feel right. When answering the phone, I was still slurring my words. I knew something was wrong. I had a coworker take me to the closest hospital. My dad met me there. My blood pressure was scary high. I believe it was around 200/160. They gave me Ativan and when my blood pressure lowered, they released me and told me to go home. The following day, something *still* didn't feel right. I was having severe tingling and discomfort in my left arm disrupting my sleep the previous night. My mom told me to go to another hospital which was down the street from my house. There, they gave me an MRI and discovered I had suffered a transient ischemic attack, or a mini-stroke as many refer to it. It was due to unexplained hypertension. However, I was pretty sure I knew the explanation. I still suffered from multiple eating disorders. I would restrict my food intake for days and then binge on other days. I was not taking care of my body. I was put on even more medication which made me feel embarrassed and ashamed. How many thirty-year-olds do you know taking hypertension medication? I'm still on this medication, but I've learned to give myself a break since then.

Chapter 14

Suicide Round Two

I met another guy in the spring of '18. He was cute and successful, and he had a boat! We dated for four months until he went to rehab for alcoholism. I was willing to stand by him. I looked after his dog while he was there, and then shortly after that he broke up with me. He blamed it on his sponsor.

So at this point, I'm still getting plenty of validation that I am not loveable, men are not trustworthy, and they will always leave me. I handled that breakup pretty well. I had gotten used to disappointment, and I knew what to expect living single. It was Banjo and me against the world. However, I still had issues with depression, and about a year after that breakup, my medication was all out of whack. The thing they don't discuss about mental illness is that there's no miracle drug combination for each person. You can find the perfect combination of meds, but the brain's chemistry is constantly changing. What works for me one day could completely change without a moment's notice. So depression started sneaking in. As per usual, I didn't tell anyone. I just thought I could fight it off.

On Easter of 2019, I spent the day with my dad and stepmom, along with my brother and his family. When I came home, I took about thirty Ativan pills and chased them down with a bottle of champagne. No one expected it. There were literally zero outward signs that I was suicidal.

So imagine my surprise at waking up the next morning, well past time to be at work, to the sound of my phone ringing. I answered. It was my mom. She was hysterical. She had been called by my HR representative, who knew about my history with mental illness and had alerted my mom when work couldn't get a hold of me.

I looked around and didn't recognize my surroundings. My bedroom table was upside down in the kitchen. The bathroom curtain and curtain rod were on the floor of my bedroom, and I had bruises up and down my body. My poor Banjo was underneath my bed. God only knows what terror he went through that night, watching me do whatever it was that I did. I still have zero recollection. All I knew was that I was alive, and my mom was now knocking on my door.

She helped me pack a bag and took me back to her house. Her husband, Rob, followed us in my car. I didn't tell my mom about my suicide attempt because I didn't want to be committed to the psychiatric unit. I tried to go to work the following day, but I ran over a curb in the parking lot and got a flat tire. That just blew everything up. My amazing boss told me I should go home. My HR rep strongly recommended I go get help. It was right then and there that I decided I needed real psychiatric help. My mom came and picked me up, and I finally told her about my suicide attempt. She insisted I get treatment at a local mental health center.

Chapter 15

Recovery

It was at the treatment center that I met my sister, Arianna. She is one of the reasons I am still here and writing about this now. She is exactly like I was at her age (twenty-one at the time). I have been able to do so much healing through mentoring her, and she has been just as inspirational and supportive to me.

This time around, I knew it had to be different. This wasn't going to be just another point in my vicious cycles. That was it. That was the last rock bottom. Now I had someone who depended on me. Someone I needed to be alive for. I finally started seeing a therapist that scares the shit out of me, but it's because he makes me uncomfortable. He has helped me with my illogical thoughts and male attention issues and has helped me learn how to live my life day to day as well as to look ahead and see a future.

It was through therapy and joining support groups for survivors of the troubled teen industry that I was able to come to terms with some of my root issues. So many of my insecurities, my illogical thoughts and beliefs, stemmed from Spring Creek Lodge. That is where I learned that everything, including my sexual assault and subsequent trauma, was my fault, something I should be "accountable" for. That is where I began to believe that I was a lazy, selfish, badly behaved child. That is where I acquired my extreme body-image issues and eating disorders. It was a machine for breaking down children and young adults and turning them into shells of who they once were.

These places are still out there. The troubled teen industry is a multi-billion-dollar industry. Spring Creek Lodge shut down, but it popped back up under a different name, and these programs keep spawning similar off-shoots based on the same disgusting principals and abusive tactics.

If my parents had known I was mentally ill, I could've been saved from this torture camp, but mental illness was a taboo subject then, much like it is today. Thankfully now it is being talked about more, and studies have advanced the science of mental illness by leaps and bounds.

However, we're still not where we need to be with mental health awareness and acceptance. There are so many people suffering in silence and feeling desperately alone, people who are scared to seek help and scared to admit they are sick. That's why I'm speaking out. I'm speaking out on behalf of survivors of the troubled teen industry but also for those who suffer from mental illness. We will suffer silently no longer. I will protest the institutions that broke me, and I will scream my struggles with mental illness from the rooftops.

I am a survivor. I am a warrior. I am loved, and I am worthy. All I want to do is help others feel the same.